In the Desert

Greater Palm Springs, CA
February 2018

Travelers in the Desert
Dry and arid land
Learning to adapt

A journal
by **Sue k Green**

Printed in the United States of America

Published March 2018

Available on Amazon;com and other retailers

ISBN-13:978-1986541602

ISBN-10:1986541606

Table of Contents

Travel Journal: February 6-12, 2018

Dedicated to my travel companions.

Palm Springs lies on the western edge of the Coachella Valley, within the Colorado Desert, located approximately 110 miles southeast of Los Angeles and 140 miles northeast of San Diego. The geography of Palm Springs is what creates the famed warm, dry climate. At 487 feet above sea level, Palm Springs is sheltered by the Little San Bernardino Mountains to the north, the Santa Rosa Mountains on the south, and the San Jacinto Mountains to the west. Palm Springs has more than 350 days of sunshine with less than 5 inches of rain. Winter temperatures average in the 70's with nights in the mid-40's. However, the relentless sun, little water, and summer temperatures above 100 degrees can make a forbidding world for non-desert dwellers.

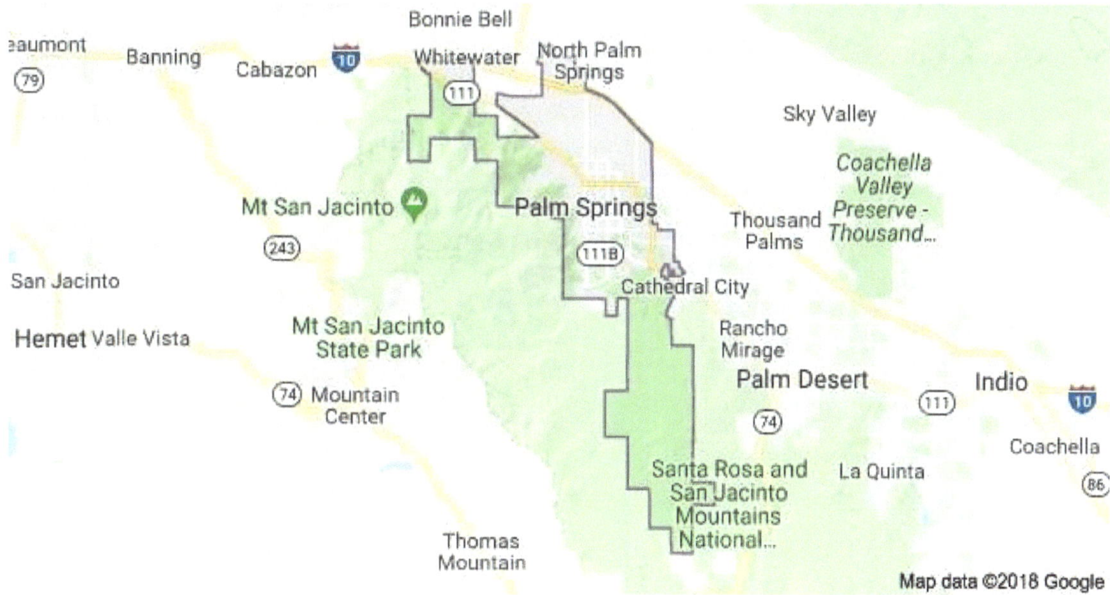

We chose to stay at the Homewood Suites in Palm Desert, a very convenient and comfortable choice for our desert travels.

There is so much to learn about the desert, and the life within. It is amazing how hundreds of species have adapted ways to conserve moisture and beat the heat in fascinating ways. Here is an amazing ecosystem where spiny cacti and succulent plant life have adjusted to the extremes of desert clime. The desert has its own food chain. Rodents, insects and lizards eat the plants, larger animals eat the smaller, and bugs feed off the dead. In years past, many indigenous groups learned to live off the land, even drinking water found in the fleshy parts of cactus. We see only signs that desert animals have left behind; their adaptive behavior finds them out only when the sun goes down.

Roads curve and dip as we travel through the **San Jacinto Mountain Range**; the mountains differ in size, color, and composition, some appear to be huge piles of soil covered with sparse vegetation, others shaped by weathered stone, while others are layered with sharp edged rocks.

The **San Andrea Fault** is perhaps one of the best known, and most menacing geological features in North America, an oft-blamed continental rift responsible for plenty of earthquakes in California.

We walk the two-mile **San Andreas Canyon Trail**, breathe in the hot, dry air arid air, drink plenty of water, and take careful steps on the hard packed path beneath a cloudless sky and blazing sun.

4

The **Palm Springs Aerial Tramway**—the world's largest rotating tram car—travels over two-and-one-half miles along the cliffs of Chino Canyon, transporting visitors to the pristine wilderness of the Mt. San Jacinto State Park and Wilderness Area. During this ten-minute journey, tram cars rotate slowly, offering spectacular vistas of the valley below.

The view at the top can stretch northward for more than 200 mi on a clear day, all the way to Mount Charleston north of Las Vegas, Nevada. Views to the east and west can stretch as far as California's Salton Sea is plainly visible to the southeast.

Having reached the Tram's Mountain Station atop the 8,526 foot mountain, we lunched in one of the two restaurants while enjoying the spectacular views. There are over 50 miles of trails in the San Jacinto State Park. We chose to hike the **Desert View trail**

This trail was not well marked and I became separated from my friends. I had to depend on other hikers to find my way back to Mountain Station.

I became concerned when I did not find my friends back at Mountain Station. Many anxious moments, and several pages later, we were reunited and together we returned by tram to the foot of the mountain.

Our next stop was the **Thousand Palms Oasis**, where we found tall palms, welcome shade, and a reflecting pond. An Oasis, is a fertile tract of land that occurs in a desert wherever perennial supply of fresh water is available. Oases vary in size, ranging from about 2.5 acres around small springs to vast areas of naturally watered or irrigated land. Underground water sources account for most oases; their springs and wells, some of them artesian, are supplied from sandstone aquifers whose intake areas may be more than 500 miles away.

The Moorten Botanical Gardens, is an interesting plant nursery jam-packed with hundreds of cactus and other succulents labeled with plant names.

Also found are some old rusted coal mining relics, pulleys and wheels, just begging to be photographed.

The **Salton Sea** formed in 1905 when the flooding Colorado River accidentally diverted into the Salton Sink creating a fresh water lake filled with fish and covering the entire valley with teeming wildlife. It was developed into a recreation area. Now, a landlocked complex of faults, hills, and ancient drainages and home to millions of migrating birds, it is slowly losing a race for life due to increasing salinization. In talking to the rangers about the future of this beautiful sea and recreation area, we learn that local preservationists are now fighting a war against time hoping to preserve at least some of the area as wetlands for as long as possible.

We spot many beautiful birds along the waterfront.

Following a short trail around part of the lake, we walk on a beach that is composed, not of sand, but of skeletal remains from fish that once swam in the waters.

The **Erosion Road Drive** leads us east from Borrego
Spring through Anza-Borrego's most dynamic landscape,
where geologic forces are evident as the Coyote and Santa
Rosa Mountains stretch, shift, weather, and erode. The
land is still active with seismic changes, and with the
opposing forces of weathering, and erosion, the land has
been uplifted and exposed in the Borrego Badlands,
forming canyons, alluvial fans, exposing sedimentary
layers.

Congress has designated nearly 558,000 acres of **Joshua Tree National Park** as wilderness. Geological faults crisscross the park area and most of the park away from road corridors is wilderness. Fan Palm Oases form atop cracks in the earth's crust where ground water hits a fault and rises to the surface nourishing lush vegetation.

The park is an ecological melting pot, a transition zone. The Colorado and Mojave Deserts overlap the Colorado and Mojave Deserts, each area exhibiting very different characteristic land and native fauna, a vibrant landscape featuring plants and animals representative of both.

The eastern half lies below 3000 feet above sea level within the Colorado Desert where Creosote, spidery ocotillo, green barked palo verde, and cholla cactus can be found.

In the western half, above 3000 feet, is found a Mojave Desert habitat of yucca and prickly pear cactus, tall feathery sprays of Parry's nolina, skeletal black brush, and hundreds of wild-armed Joshua trees. One would think the many black brush plants were dead, having lost leaves in winter, but I understand this is normal and they are very much alive.

A large area beyond this point is 'designated wilderness,' where the earth and its community of life are protected and visitors are not allowed to trespass.

In the Western Half of the park are hundreds and hundreds of Joshua trees, amazingly different in shape and size.

We drove for miles past this **Wind Farm on the San Gorgonio Mountain Pass** in the San Bernadino Mountains. We learned later that it contains more than 4000 separate windmills and provides enough electricity to power Palm Springs and the entire Coachella Valley.

If you enjoyed this journal, you may be interested in ***"Exploring Paths of the Past"*** with this author/photographer as she documents her 2014 visit to New Mexico, Arizona, and Utah.